G000055090

The
Darling
North

The Darling North

ANNE KENNEDY

AUCKLAND
UNIVERSITY
PRESS

for Robert

First published 2012

Auckland University Press
University of Auckland
Private Bag 92019
Auckland 1142
New Zealand
www.press.auckland.ac.nz

© Anne Kennedy, 2012

ISBN 978 1 86940 593 9

Publication is kindly assisted by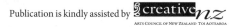

National Library of New Zealand Cataloguing-in-Publication Data
Kennedy, Anne, 1959-
The darling north / Anne Kennedy.
ISBN 978-1-86940-593-9
I. Title.
NZ821.3—dc 23

This book is copyright. Apart from fair dealing for the purpose of private study,
research, criticism or review, as permitted under the Copyright Act, no part may
be reproduced by any process without prior permission of the publisher.

Versions of these poems have appeared in *Southerly*, *Turbine*, *Landfall*, *Sport*,
The Page, *Home & Away* (nzepc), *Best New Zealand Poems*, *Poetry New Zealand* and
Big Weather: Poems of Wellington, edited by Gregory O'Brien and Louise St John.

Cover image: Megan J. Campbell, *Here There and Everywhere* (details), 2007, oil on canvas.
Photograph by Silver Image Photography

Cover design: Keely O'Shannessy

Printed in China by 1010 Printing International Ltd

It was a beautiful place – wild, untouched, above all untouched, with an alien, disturbing, secret loveliness. And it kept its secret. I'd find myself thinking, 'What I see is nothing – I want what it hides *– that is not nothing.'*
– *Jean Rhys,* Wide Sargasso Sea

CONTENTS

THE DARLING NORTH

*I have now all New Zealand before me to caper about in; so I shall
do as I like, and please myself. I shall keep to neither rule, rhyme,
nor reason, but just write what comes uppermost to my recollec-
tion of the good old days. – F. E. Maning,* Old New Zealand

A Land Court

I woke in the morning when the clock dusted its hands
after an untidy night-time. Lips fluttered

travel plans into my back. My ribcage reverberated
like a cello. He had land so I called him Maning.

We were going up north, the thing to do
down here in the hemisphere.

I'd never looked at landscapes, only heard them,
which was safer, the ear a sieve for

devastation. I liked hubbub, how our apartment
undid the city like a corkscrew. A globe

webbed with lat. and long. and the tracks of former lovers
quivered in one corner. Every so often Maning or I

gave the Tropic of Capricorn a flick, exposing
the soft underside of the other, and the South Seas.

It was a disused schoolhouse in the Hokianga, a hang-out.
I'd been nearby, remembered mudflats, flatness,

nothing much, soundtracks mostly.
I had a compass. I'd had a friend (she moved to England)

who said you should always sleep pointing due north.
It sounded feasible. Finding her waterbed too big to shift

she slept crosswise, fitfully, due to the uncomfortable overhang
of her ankles. Maning and I favoured a clock tower.

All through the night bells rang changes. Half-waking,
I felt them in my heart and in my lungs. In sunlight

I lay close to the coiled hairs on his legs, degrees
Celsius, a cast in my eye, and I lived there

small, below decks. I liked the hardness
of his thighs compared with my own. They were landowners,

his people, crops, sheep, but what I discovered was
if there were no women in the world

he would starve to death. That's how the line
would die out. He was an artist: ideas, paint.

I once toppled through a sliding door he'd just cracked
a nut in. It jumped off its hinges. We lay on the bed,

rolls of dust under it: a childhood
belief that was where souls went and where they'd

come from. Air-born. Some afternoons
I mopped there and shook out the dead souls

into the wind above the clock tower. Evenings
I worked in a cardboard room, rather crowded, finding

mistakes in the newspaper. It was jovial – the proofreaders'
jokes, their anecdotes, although night was day

and up down. When the phone rang a subeditor's voice
was drenched in sunshine. After midnight

I'd find Maning with his pen dipped in a pool of rainwater
turned black by the action of many nights upon it,

drawing figures, scarved friends who bopped their heads
to the blues, to vinyl, vodka, moonlight. It got later

despite the clocks, which ticked towards the shores
of the Hokianga, and the weekend.

The friends said oh you'll love the north,
and not just north, Far North. The tip. Maning agreed:

Everyone goes north. I had listened to northness,
a hiss, a crackle, a buckle of air.

Auckland howled. A clock gonged at night, and at dawn
a bulldozer sorted the chunks

of a dream. I'd bought the alarm clock
so I could wake up in the morning. Maning took it,

set it every night for an obscure hour. At 8.23 a.m.
I blinked at his inventiveness, the way his hand

extended from his sleeve. I'd run my fingers
over my face to be sure of it. When we got to the land,

the disused schoolhouse on the shores of the Hokianga,
I would mop its floors. The night before

he is moving inside my body when the telephone rings.
At first I think it's the clock tower.

It rings and rings. By thirty rings he has shrunk away,
gone naked to answer the greater urge.

I lie on the bed watching him, my body like strewn hay
(I imagine). He replies yes to a question and laughs

into the receiver. *A love-nest is disturbed.*
Back in bed he says his friend from France (from the long.)

flies in and out dans le weekend. We'll be up north,
he says, so I'll miss her. He'll miss her

in the Hokianga. No no, I say, we don't have to go.
Oh we do, he says. We don't. (The deliberations.)

Shall we go north? No. *Shall we go north? No!*
We would stay in the south.

Stretch of Hokianga

His name by some stretch of the imagination is Stretch
and he lives with his parents in a little house

on the southern reaches of the Hokianga.
In a hundred years there's been small change

in the land,
the silver-dollar harvest of the Moreton Bay figs,

in the movements of the family
apart from the sandspit spend by the sea, a brother dipped

over the hill, they are keeping everything
just as it was. But lately, to make ends meet,

Stretch has taken weekend tenants. Friday evenings
are hilarious with car horns.

An uncle owned it. It stood on his ripped-off bit
of the family plot, biggest house on the Hokianga Harbour,

eighteen rooms at low tide. Being a bachelor, childless,
as is the wont of uncles, he left

the house to Stretch, younger brother, because the elder
had gone marae. Married. There were so many.

It's two-storeyed, wide-pillared, veranda attended by
Norfolk pines, a cypress thinner and more brooding,

wine bottles crooked in its arms,
banana palms shredded like important documents.

From the road at night, the house lit up,
a hundred diners rattle their knives and forks

and shake their frilly sleeves. In the house it's just Stretch
operating a circular saw. Weeknights he renovates.

On Fridays he bumps home to his parents' bungalow
across the valley, leaves the tenants

lugging their coffee-maker, their water-purifier. The tide
is stirred as it changes. They're professional girls

in the book trade, perhaps jilted. Stretch watches
in the rearview mirror as they drape the veranda

5

with ragged wedding dresses.
Once he told the lessee, a nice woman called Barbara,

he would like to live in the eighteen-roomed house with his wife,
whom he has not had the good fortune to meet yet.

(He is tall of course.) There are no eligible women
in the district. They all go to Auckland. His eyes

reflect all the blueness in the sky leaving the Hokianga
to silver. Later lights sit

in the cypresses, ghosts stalk the halls. He doesn't like
to think. He knows his history,

the way the north pulled his forebears (the Fortunes)
south with the moon, and on a neap tide

they entered the mouth. Coughed up
diddly-squat (said Barbara

later) through the Land Court. Clutching a document
and a cattle station, they called it Oke Hanga,

built a veranda'd house in the vicinity of a church, a pa,
flour-mill, fish-canning factory, a sprinkling

of cottages and a schoolhouse
for their many children, little north in the south

but better, better. They'd been peasants
in the true north, in the lemon-coloured last night,

and now they were squires. (Maning by the way
thinks the treaty should be ratified. His family land sits

on the land.) I'd never lived with strangers
but after six months cohabitating with the ghost of a man

who had left taking everything with him apart from
his presence which still hung in the wardrobe,

lay folded in drawers and beside me at night
making me gasp,

I also packed up and departed, moved in with
two women in the book trade. Monday to Friday,

dressing-gowns, wings, on the way to the bathroom.
In the weekend I met them: Barbara, Issy,

told me they hawked advance copies in the south.
Nice to meet you, they said, let's go north. Remember

The Navigator, when the boy shuts his eyes in order to see?
I soon found myself on the shores of the Hokianga

on the edge of a weekend
in the house next door to the disused schoolhouse,

Maning's (*my* Maning), that we planned to stay in
but we never did. Now I go north with

Barbara and Issy because you go north.
In my black car I buzz the coast like an insect. I watch

the mudflats hold the tide, quivering, indecisive,
until finally as if going back

for its dove jacket, the water floods in . . . *and so,*
putting on the most unconcerned countenance possible,

I prepared to make my entrée *into Maori land*
in a proper and dignified manner.

The Fortunes bred a family of twins, something in the gregarious
nature of their genes. Three died all at once,

one and a half sets, an accident at sea, they're buried over the hill.
It is perhaps for this reason – the finality of land,

the fickleness of people – that Stretch advertised in the *Herald*
for tenants rather than live in the house himself.

Nothing secure but the permanence of newspapers.
(In the warm room someone proofread

his ad for errors, perhaps me. There was deliberation
over reaches or beaches, northern or southern.)

It was a hot Christmas Day, the last of the hot Christmases
seemingly, because after that the floods came.

In the morning a man came to the door with a key for Barbara.
I answered. They'd come from Oke Hanga,

a car full of kids, scorched as fillet. We're a bit
hung-over, he said, it's your turn.

I took the key in the palm of my hand. It made an imprint,
the long way. The next day it rained. It rained

all summer long. We drove through the torrents, white
like washday. Barbara, Issy, their friends in the book trade,

and me, because I was love flotsam.
We went north because everyone went north.

It was Boxing Day and people flooded into the rooms,
lay in the shallow multitudinous beds

and ran up and down the stairs which were carpeted
in green tartan as if it were Balmoral.

I took them two at a time.
Outside it rained down on *the slime kingdoms*.

I had never looked at land or given landscape the time of day,
wanting nothing of this land or of this light,

of the unthreading of Auckland as its beads rolled
due north. Now that I hated him,

his inventiveness, his thighs, I could walk
in the warm north, inoculated, the chances infinitesimal

of ink-rash or dust attack, of an amoeba or old record
finding me. I could walk among northness,

touching it, its leaves, water, movement.
Like everyone, I would see north.

Barbara is the only one among us who has met the brother.
Once he came to the gate, gun slung over one arm,

peered at Stretch replacing boards on the veranda.
Barbara asked would your brother

9

like to come in for a cup of tea to which Stretch replied
no he would not.

A Signature

His sleeve, or the prevailing wind from these sleeves,
one afternoon brushed his disastrous love life

onto the carpet where it made a dark stain. He was minding
a house in the crook of Waitemata, Auckland,

its owner home in England. At that moment
she looked down involuntarily at the footpath in Sloane Square.

He reached for an afternoon's drawings to mop up the mess,
on hand on a roll in the kitchen. When people visited

he ripped off volleys of naked women to lie in their laps
while they ate takeaways, to mark with the imprint

of lipstick before they left. This was the way he talked,
not me. I visited the house at low tide.

I could tell a flow of vanilla had been there by the objects
beached at the high-water mark,

his abandoned jandals, a sweetness, too much talk, nothing left
unsaid – well, I hid things sometimes.

He told me everything he knew only leaving out the things
he had chosen not to know. Paths go down

to the sea through the suburban bush. He'd learnt them off by heart
acquiring a knowledge of these parts like a London cabbie.

I followed. He raced ahead, retrieved his jandals from the edge
of the ink stain. I tried not to be drawn. The sugar works

on the bay hummed like a small orchestra. Bags billowing
with confection destined for England

were being loaded onto a barge and sent across the harbour
to the port of Auckland. Behind it

the business district, the courts, the hotels flickered like handwriting.
The harbour stirred, edgy from being watched.

I said I was going to the Hokianga for the weekend.
My life without him sounded interesting.

I told him I'd been dating in his absence, met a man,
not true, but thought he was very nice,

talked about him the way a man talks about a woman:
great legs. Maning says

you think I have everything but in a way I have nothing.
Under no circumstances would I be drawn.

Later we kissed or ate
against the banister. That day I talked in

sentences no more than four inches long.
When he shows me the remains of the ink stain

I want to get down on my hands and knees and lick
the last dark translation from the carpet

because I love his disasters – earth, minerals, fluids,
I want the smudge on my tongue.

His mother, he says, and other admirers have suggested applying
fuller's earth, vanilla essence, milk, to the stain.

Knowledge. At that point I flee home to my beloved
grief. The owner of the house will return from England

to find the piles of her house matted
from where he has been at them with a wire brush.

He will clear away all trace of what was there before
but not without drawing me in. What I realise,

as my black car copperplates over the bridge, is
love makes the land appear and disappear.

Evidence from the Veranda

In the end there is nowhere to go but back to the Hokianga.
It is summer but it rains every day. Friday evening

the party walks out in gumboots to a lake a mile away
blown in half by the prevailing northerly pushing

its cover of pale green slime to one side. It appears suddenly
in the landscape like a neenish tart. We trail

along the beach in drizzle to meet the nearest neighbour,
a man from Auckland who apparently

inherited the schoolhouse, the disused schoolhouse.
I know it will be empty.

The hydrangeas are ludicrous. The criss-cross balustrade,
polite keep-out, invites me up

to the ochre veranda. It's sanded bare, beveled. The foreshore
is taking it back. My palms make

safety glasses. Little desks, row of hooks, dead fireplace.
Dust bunnies rush helter-skelter.

We hurry away before the incoming tide cuts off our access
which would force us to use the long looping road,

and nobody wants to. Across the sludgy inlet
the late sun is fizzy with rain. We stop at the marae

and talk to a man leaning on a toothy fortification. You fellas
down from Auckland? Yes yes, from Auckland,

but up. Up. He talks in waves about the district,
mounds, mouth, flat, forest. Or used to be.

He bats across the water at the schoolhouse. Shut up
shop during the Depression, sold into private title.

A Pakeha farmer won it one drunken night of cards, 1935.
Still in the family, seldom there.

Back at Oke Hanga someone builds a fire, open as in naked.
On the lawn, derelict playground equipment rocks

to and fro in the gathering storm as if enormous grey children
play on it, branches caught in their hair. Barbara

says the house was once converted into a children's home.
That's why there are so many

little rooms. (Stretch is gradually knocking down
the flimsy walls.) Barbara would like to write a monograph:

the house and environs, its history. History
of the north, its future,

13

the house restored, empty during the week save for Stretch and his
phantom wife, their bed blown about on wild nights

from room to room. In the weekends
they give it over to the party in the book trade,

their children and their children's children's books.
How nomadic they are! Read *The Songlines*, spend two weeks

out of three in motels in the upper North Island,
on Friday nights at Oke Hanga

thankfully climb the tartan stairs to bed. One weekend
everyone will drive up to the tip, the northern-most point

where the Pacific and the Tasman shake hands, goodbye,
and souls jump off because there is no more north.

I had a forebear, apparently, manned the lighthouse
up there. Did I say that? And his wife and children.

At Oke Hanga the porch is as big as an apartment I rented,
half with a lover, half alone, blown apart

like the lake. The dining table seats twenty for dinner, it's strewn
with advance copies of books, a stuffed Penguin,

the claws of the wind, the sky gleaming
down on it. In the small south

hours, the party is drawn like sand
to the bedrooms. My room is big – sky, sea, light,

pressed into a straw-coloured cube. Big bed, little else
apart from the coming and going of net curtains

leaving a tidemark on the carpet. One weekend when there is
nothing else to do we will all drive to Cape Reinga.

Also a colony of bees in the wall – low-pitched drone at night,
in the mornings their coffee-crystal hour-glass figures hovering.

Once I heard a man say this to his mate on the bus:
she's got an hour-glass figure

only all the sand's gone to one end. At dinner (the big table)
we were talking about trees and Ian said

without trees there would be no bestsellers.
Pinus contorta, which grows thickly in all directions,

is becoming a problem at the military camp in Waiouru.
The army, rather than chop down the trees,

used them for target practice. And every splinter
formed a new tree. Maning is in Auckland,

his schoolhouse dark, and I am as far north as possible
without jumping off

into the place where the two famous seas meet
and sign a treaty endlessly in blue and turquoise.

In the end there was nowhere else to go.
There is wine and talk of the funny forebears, peculiar,

you could tell by their sepia expressions and the stories
circulating. Mine

exiled by the Potato Famine – the Famine
had a thing about them, infidels

in the kingdom of starvation. They stepped gingerly
(redheads) onto the new land,

but kept their down-at-heel shoes on, scared to earth themselves
into the warm soil

which might be *sowed with the mouthing corpses*
of six hundred papists. Wasn't, only with the tendrils

of potatoes. Got jobs then, for instance
in the telegraphic section of the Post Office, dealing with

displacement. Regret to inform in dash-dot-dot. They hurled
the babies' afterbirths

into hospital incinerators. The smoke furled, floated
and looked down at the bodies

moving about on the gun-metal hills, the unanswering sky,
their little lives

tumbleweed on the Desert Road. The land
hated them. How I know this: I don't. Don't

listen to me. There are two roads to Oke Hanga, Burley Road
and the other way. Issy decides to walk

the fifteen Ks in from the main road for the heck of it,
sets off with a red pack and a Walkman.

Maning earthed me, a brown
wire. I became an in-law of the land.

Did you know Brahms copied out chunks of Beethoven
and inserted them in his symphonies.

He said Beethoven's music is mine
because I love him. All weekend

I watch the tide come and go from the misty veranda,
a coincidence. A couple of times

go out for walks with various people, Barbara,
mud knee-high. In the middle of the night

Sarah raps on my door and says listen to the rustle of silk
promenading up and down the hall.

I can't hear a thing, I murmur, apart from his ghost
and the photographs, and the bees in the wall.

In the time of the Fortunes, says Barbara (who will write a monograph),
the mill was propelled by divine motion, ghostly,

ticking of the sky, singing in the church,
stories of home, three trees on the hill. Someone

has slalomed into the village for milk and newspapers,
passed Issy on the road. An hour later she appears pale

at Oke Hanga, her new red pack bled all over her back.
I've done it, she says. (*It is*

accomplished.) That day Stretch stayed up at the bungalow.
In the afternoon it cleared. Flies milled

17

in the middle of the room. You'll shuffle the spots off them,
said Barbara to the dealer. Sitting out on the veranda

under a brass plaque. At one stage I twisted around to look at it.
We went swimming. It was summer. A Plunket nurse

wouldn't go in because of harbour germs.
The skin of the water hid the commotion

of the immigrants, the scarring of ships. Ian took
his kite down to the beach, a giant sperm, fifty-metre tail,

I had a go and felt the strange delight
of something tugging at you.

Northness

1 a.m. in my bedroom a bright line like phosphorous radiates
under the balcony doors. The north wants to come in.

But I – with my new friends my new hate my new northness –
am going to it. I step past the humming of bees

onto the high lacy veranda. I wear my nightdress, a south dress,
snowy and windy. It flutters at all angles, is melted

by the north. Across the dissenting heads of the pines
the harbour turns over in its sleep. I think

it is sleeping. I see its dream, its wrinkling. I am bathed
in blueness and the harbour is leached of blue.

There's an ache just here, a siren in my lungs,
high-pitched so you can't hear it

but in the distance a dog whines. Down on the lawn
among the swings and slides dark shadows like legs

flee somewhere, I don't know where, but I am beginning
to wonder. I hear laughing downstairs, happiness.

I am facing the greyed Hokianga and the delicate fact
that Maning did not exist, at least not in the way

I had imagined. The retreating tide has taken its power,
and left stones, wood, shoes. (*No treaty*

I foresee will salve completely your tracked
and stretchmarked body . . .)

I put my coat on over my nightdress and navigate
the trembling upper veranda, its nervous

kauri planks penned like wild horses under my feet
and I bounce down the foaming moonlit steps

to the garden, where a cat scallops, and a hedgehog
snuffles obliquely into flax. It is cool.

Moonlight floods on and off, a tap, when clouds allow
or the wind allows. Periodically the land leaps

up at me, whiteness, and the wide semi-tropical leaves
like emissaries, resined with recent rain, helmeted,

and I snort, my heart relentless like the water cycle.
Northness has overcome me. I am warm

as I walk over it, finding paths in the sprays of grass,
in the low desperate bushes, in the tough busy

bacteria of the soil. In the dark I see shots, blades, edges,
and they guide me, and among the foliage, in the air,

under the echoing mauve shell of the sky that cups
over the harbour, I plot my course

like a whale listening to its own springy co-ordinates.
I am acquiring the knowledge. All night (it seems) I walk

in the disused landscape. At one point it rains again
and I am drenched, slippery as if newborn.

I'm not, of course, I am recycled, derivative –
my long immigrant upper lip, my blue postal-worker eyes,

white skin caught occasionally in the moonlight,
face flipped open like a passport.

My ID stares out. Here I am,
like Maning (who I think of with a jolt at this moment –

this moment – in the untidy night-time). I have hereness,
at least evidence of it. They

had nothing, that lot (the forebears, them again),
but dash-dot, air, whiteness, ships passing

the mouth of the harbour with a sack of flour. The sugar
settled their teeth. They never complained

(from the sit-still photographs), but made do, made
bodies. The northness made them do it,

I think. The warmth, the lushness, the wild fertility,
is what they came south for.

The night bruises. Under my feet the tidal flat gurgles,
an invisible city, worm farms.

I look down: *mother ground
sour with the blood of her faithful.* I scuff back to the house

in my coat. The land is slabs of meat, blocks of butter, angled
for the taking. I could reach down.

In the meantime, the night-time, the sky ticks, the steps gleam,
the house creaks. I sleep listening to bees.

Off and on the next day I shave trees, shading my eyes
with my visor hand as I scan the horizon.

Some burnt stumps surprise me in a field. I delve
into the mud hoping to find bright yellow fists

of glassiness. There are none. All gone, all
glue. I read in the big front room (they have everything,

Barbara, Issy, Ian, all the books). I read while the harbour
watches me. Wars, uprisings, skirmishes,

quashed, undone, done. What am I to do with it? A painting,
Entrance of the E-O-Ke-Angha River, Augustus Earle,

is squirts of milk-light, smeared, coaxed, hovering even
over the canvas, painted in a trance, under some

influence. My feet, when I walk out again, are six inches
above clay. I plant the north in history books. They go crazy

in the unaccustomed warmth. *I can hardly understand
how it is that I have not yet landed.*

21

At eight o'clock on Sunday the party goes from room to room
closing windows, although there is no one

to come in. Only Stretch rollercoasting over the hills
with his circular saw. Everyone

has orange hair in the end, and a bright frown
from the low sun. I watch

my love being sucked up from the harbour, from the land
then falling again, quite gently.

One day, says Barbara, we will drive up to the northern-most
point and look out at the two seas.

I lock the rumbling sash in the room with bees. The milk curtains
go still, but the tirade of water through the warped glass

billows back into the inlet.
The bees continue with their deliberations. I am north

in the south. *I get so confused. I feel just as if I was
two different persons at the same time.*

From now on in conversations about the north
I will describe the harbour I saw, its wild silence.

In convoy the party drives back south, Barbara and Issy,
Ian, Sarah, me, etc. A song in my black car

floats on the darkening air. I turn the headlights on
at Wellsford, baubles, going south.

The hills rock, the motorway roars, birds fly out
from neon signs, European trade beads flung into the sky.

In Auckland under the imported lemon
lamp-post, Barbara and Issy load up their cars

for Monday morning. They will drive books in every direction
but it will all be in the south. Monday evening

I will be in the flimsy reading room. The phone will ring
and I will answer its daylight.

I have buried my history, my lost love in the tidal flat.
One day I will drive up or down

to the northern-most point and look out and up and back
at the north.

HANDS ON: A HANDBOOK

<u>Case 1: The Pinkish Wine</u>

1a

Grandma was sick as a dog. Ruby said, I'll go.
A supermarket bag ticked with six cakes.
You think, said Mum, I'd let my only daughter

walk those woods alone? A spare
daughter might have fared differently
if she'd existed.

Mum put in a bottle of Chablis, no
rosé on second thoughts, for
Grandma's afternoon tea.

1b

Sure enough on the path, a wolf.
Sick too, as it happened, sick as a human.
A morsel, he whined, a drink, not too much to ask,

is it? Mum scared him off
with her famous fireplace snarl, white dust
on her tongue, evidence of something lacking,

a letter. The wolf slunk off, his fluffy tail between
a broom and a boy's pocket-knifed toetoe.

Mum called after him, Don't think you've got the monopoly
on warm-blooded and furry, Mister.
To Ruby: I can play

the female-defending-young card. Mum and Ruby
continued on their way unhindered by anything apart from
Ruby's MP3 player. The Ramones

on a leash, light slatting in through the young pines
which made you think of all the previous occasions of sunlight.
Good thing I came along, said Mum. Considering

history. Ruby oblivious. Mum was
a film star with music tapping her on the shoulder
(Oh incidentally) if only she could hear it.

It got annoying after a while
for Ruby (and for us).

1c

Insects under Mum and Ruby's feet flew up from the forest floor,
This is Your Life, a cloud
of episodes. Then fell gently

to biting. Fantails followed like paparazzi
that ate the insects that swallowed

the blood. Ruby and Mum walked on towards Grandma's house
swatting the things and the path
with the soles of their shoes.

1d

At Grandma's Grandma looked a terrible colour,
and was,

the house cluttered like a palette, her ornaments,
her collection of fine dusts.
Mum said,

How are you anyway? out the side of her mouth like smoking,
a bad habit, all these years.
Never you mind how I am, said Grandma, I just am,
nothing you can do about it.

That's a bit rich considering, said Mum,
the visit, the cakes, their faces (the round things).

And the wine. Let's drink to the wine.
Well all right I'll drink to that.
And they drank

1e

except Ruby who had two cakes, and
when Grandma asked her to go and get the whisky she had
a walk to the cabinet to get the whisky.

Presently Grandma said,
The Prime Minister is coming this afternoon. Helen.
Mum clicked her tongue over and over, a twig

in bike spokes.
Jesus (in fact talking to Ruby), not these
delusions of grandeur again! Grandma was

wounded. I didn't say *I* was the Prime Minister.
Did I Ruby?
No, said Ruby.

She'll be here at three o'clock, said Grandma.
Mum looked sly. I thought you said you were sick.
I was but now I'm better.

Jesus, we come all this way!
Ruby said, Mum, don't!
No really, all the way through the woods.

It's not woods, Mum.
Fine fine, pines. Pines.

Can I help it if your grandmother won't sell her house
to the Christmas tree company? Can I
help it if the closer it gets to December the taller the trees are –

Can I help you? said Grandma.
No.

– the taller the trees the crazier the people
sleeping under them.
Mind you who

can talk? Look. Bulbous eyes, enlarged nose, slavering teeth.
It's only the wine, said Ruby.

Years of wine, said Mum.
Mum, please!
Thank you. I'll thank you to keep out of this.

Leave then! cried Grandma. Leave and don't ever come back.
Fine.
Fine with me. Don't meet the Prime Minister.

Ruby, we're going. We're leaving and we're never
coming back. We're leaving this
basket-case.

1f

Earphone buds mating in mid-air, the new indigestible
insects.
Back through the woods. Mum on alert: watch out for
the wolf won't you.

Ruby to Mum: Mum, it's not woods and it's not wolf,
this is the Pacific. It's bush and paedophiles.
Oh I know, don't think I don't read the *Herald*.

(The white album
an anthology, the canon.)

Even more reason. I have
even more reason.

About this afternoon, I'm sorry it was all so something
but you know your grandmother –
That's all right.
– what I was going to say, so damaging.

They talked about it and they talked about it. At least we
can talk about it, damage, utter the word
damage. At least you're safe.

Yes.
A high level of safety. I was never this safe. A miracle
I'm here to tell the tale.

Case 2: Please Man

2a

The first little pig thought he'd build a house. You
mean a fort, said Dad – right you are little man (i.e., little pig).
They got up early. Dad's trotters clattered

on Trade Me. Little Pig jigged in the monitor's blue glow.
They drove out to where a beautiful pink swamp
met the highway. Dad inhaled deeply, reminds me

of the farm mornings of my youth (urea). Some Saturdays
he regretted the Wolf Studies Dept. They met the vendor
and Dad asked him if he was the vendor.
(He was a man.)

If I'm the vendor you must be the vendee. Tee hee (this is true).
The greedy car boot soon bristled. The man chewed straw
and said I would've given you that gratis if you'd asked.

Roaring off – Little Pig postmarked on the back seat –
Dad said, Be careful about men you meet on the internet son.
Dad built a twanging fort in the back yard. Little Pig did

Game Piglet. Raping six miss piggies got you a fort.
Around lunch-time a wolf flourished the gate. Ta da.
Leaned his stalactites, his sly expression, on the air

in the yard. Dad pumped wolf's hand (i.e., paw). How can I help?
Hey ho fatpork panfry, said the wolf. Good day to you, too,
said Dad. Hey ho gristlechew cracklefat.

Little Pig snouted out the window of the house (fort).
The guy's a prick, he said in Pig. Ethay uygay's ahay ickpray.
Mm, said Dad. He trottered his bristly chin. Excuse us a minute.

Ducked inside the fort (house). Little Pig,
use your tolerant words. If a pig were a man
and a wolf were a man, we'd have much in common.

I take off my hat, in a manner of speaking
or grunting. Go out there and apologise to Mister Wolf.
Little Pig saved his game. It took a while, a bus stop.

Just then the fort shook and shook. Look son, said Dad,
an example of huffing and puffing. We're lucky indeed. Rarely
have I seen such a display of traditional huff and puff behaviour.

The wolf huffed and he puffed and he h. and he p.
and he etc. etc.
and he blew the house down (i.e., fort).

Dad and Little Pig bucketed inside where Mum had
warm swill waiting in the bath. The wolf slunk off with his tail
between a broom and a boy's pocket-knifed toetoe.

2b

The next Friday Pig 2 said if houses were being handed out
he should have one. Fair enough, said Dad, but four things:
no straw no strange men no games, and it's a fort.

And no more wolves, said Little Pig. Goes without saying,
said Dad, or grunting. Crack of dawn Saturday Dad bought
wood from the cheery individual at the hardware store,

came home and woke up Pig 2, or tried to.
I'll huff and I'll puff, joked Dad. Seriously, this reminds me
of the woodworking classes of my youth. He knocked up

the fort (house) ruminating on how pigs had been
unfairly treated in primary sources such as novels (or poems)
e.g., portrayed as dogmatic farm animals even though

they weren't dogs. Get up Pig 2! I'll huff and I'll puff!
Fuck off, said Pig 2. But he lolloped into the fort (house).
Cool, he said, and lay down. His tail opened wine with each snore.

Dad hammered on, explaining about secondary sources,
articles and suchlike, which by and large, especially large,
ignored pigs. You could drive a truck through, said Dad,

the absence of pigs in critical theory. The field
is wide open, son. Grasp it with both hands (i.e., trotters).
Pig 2 slept on, the fort (house) forming around him until

he heard the tell-tale pig-squeak of the gate and a cursory
huff. He opened one eye (we think – hard to see).
Hey ho sweetsour blittymeat. Hey ho flapskillet spittyfat.

Dad drag-queened inside the fort (house), high up
and dizzy on his trotters. Pig 2 reared up too,
but like a man. I'll get him Dad. No son, don't succumb

to stereotyping – that wily hairy toothy eat-your-grandmother
stuff is about as true as pigs being fat greedy lazy victims,
with victim mentalities. Son, we're all the same,

son, student pathologists first draw juice
from an orange, then blood from a pig,
then lastly yes lastly, the bluey blood of a human.

What can we learn from that, son? Outside the wolf huffed
and he puffed and he huffed and he puffed and he.
That a man, said Pig 2, is sweet. There was then a maelstrom

of huffing and puffing. Dad's pudgy flesh pulsed
in out, in out, and on Pig 2's bristles, beads of sweat struggled
determined like little snails getting on with it.

Huff puff huff puff huff puff huff puff. Muffellous stuff,
stuttered Dad. He cuffed his Ventolin. The walls shuddered
like lungs. Run for it, son! They trotted for it

as wood became like matches and like firewood
and like pick-up sticks and like a French dessert and like
the hands of a thinking person thinking up marvellous

ideas. Inside Ma Pig made her famous warm bathtub of swill
with Everything In It, which they liked. Outside the wolf slunk off
thinking himself a clever sculptor. But he isn't, said Pig 2.

2c

The biggest little pig was Big Pig. He said ditto to Dad
re: the house, and Dad said ditto to you too, Big Pig,
but seven things: no straw no strange men no games no wood

no sleeping on the job no bad grunting, and it's a fort.
And no wolves, chorused Little Pig and Pig 2.
Oh we've seen the last of Mister Wolf, said Dad,

if I know anything about wolf behaviour.
Big Pig drove and Dad held his heart and his tongue
out to a doll's concrete jungle in perpetual sunset, pink,

red, terracotta, and on a miniature street corner
a giant spruiker bounced and Dad, who knew what to say, said
Please man, and man's eyebrows indicated a bundle of bricks.
In the car Big Pig lollygagged. Oh pu-lease man!

Back home Big Pig's rusty trowel flapped like autumn.
Dad slapped on fixer and a red wall grew and in the intervals
between slopping Dad started a conversation about

the men and the women. I know, said Big Pig, I know all this.
Big Pig had been rutting since puberty, but still he blushed.
This is why pigs are pink, all the sex conversations.

To recover Big Pig went for smoko on the side path.
Trotting back – butt squished under hoof – his little jaw dropped.
Dad was leaning against the bright brick wall puffing a joint

with the wolf. Dad made a joke about shitting bricks which
was so funny the wolf huffed and puffed. Big Pig
went inside the house (fort) to think. Dad followed.

You have to understand the wolf's worldview, said Dad.
Was it mentioned that Dad had a PhD from the University
of Warwick, Wolf Stoodies Dept. He stood wolves.

Hey ho chopspit fattycake, the wolf giggled. He half-huffed
and half-puffed. Hey ho flatbake bristcrisp. Big Pig called
out the window, Not so hot yourself. Ignore him, said Dad.

Hey ho pokepork spattyfat, said the wolf. Big Pig sniggered.
Why I oughta, he said. Hey ho panspat porkyflap, said the wolf,
and he huffed and he puffed. Why I oughta, said Big Pig.

Oughta what? said the wolf. Oughta, said Big Pig.
Don't tease Mister Wolf, said Dad. Hey ho meatpat gristletoe.
The wolf was huffing and puffing. Why I oughta, said Big Pig.

The wolf paused. Oughta what? Just oughta, said Big Pig.
The wolf scaled the roof. He huffed and he puffed
and he huffed and he stopped. Hey ho snoutmouth appleface.

Don't answer, son, said Dad. I said hey ho snoutface applegob.
Son! said Dad. Why I oughta, said Big Pig. Hey ho
hamsam mustysauce. / Why I oughta. / Hey ho spittypan

bacyrind. / Why I oughta. / Son, this is getting out of hand
or trotter. / Hey ho porkfried sweetysour. / Why I oughta. / Hey ho
schnitzelfunken gebriskenmuffin. / Get woughta! yelled Big Pig.

Little Pig and Pig 2, in the kitchen with Ma, had
just raped some piglettes. Pig 2 looked up. We gotta
get woughta. Their games went all to hell.

Hey ho chippydust snackbag. / Why I oughta. / Enough!
said Dad. He barrelled outside. Mister Wolf!
Dad clonked up on the roof. Ignore my rude son,

continue with your huffing and puffing ceremony.
Hey ho pukubun spicychops. / Why I oughta. / Hey ho
poakasmoke hangipani. / Got the woughta? shouted Big Pig.

Little Pig and Pig 2 had got the woughta. Boil it,
said Big Pig. On the roof, Dad's trotters dinged the rivets.
Mister Wolf, my apologies, take no notice.

Hey ho kunekune puhaface. / Why I oughta. / Mister Wolf! /
Hey ho pokopoko piggyfritter. / Why I oughta. / Mister Wolf!
Dad fell down the chimney, plosh into the water.

Hey ho. / Oughta. / Hey ho. / Woughta. Everything
went silent. Good job Little Pig and Pig 2 didn't know
how to do anything including build a fire.

Case 3: Cake Takes the Bus

3a

A tanned boy
sweet as syrup
curled – like a maple leaf –
one pointy limb, then another,
up from a baking sheet.
He saw through a door
blue and green
freedom, and ran for it. (I can I can.)
After him! shrieked
a little old woman
with cookie-cutter hands
to her little old man.
He snuffed a cooking show
with the remote and made
a crouching tiger
show of pursuit,
but it was hopeless.
Their grandson, visiting,
lay his corn-fed moonface
on the kitchen table:
Call that a cookie? Gimme
that dough. He tipped
Mont Saint-Mixture
onto a floured board,
pummelled and punched it,
mashed it and minced it,
rolled out and cut out
you're under arrest.
Whined the whole time
the cookie cooked.
The little old woman's

surgically attached
metal hands gnashed
the oven door open
a crack to check.
Not quite done,
she croaked, but a fist
pudgy as a boxing glove
knocked her flat. A gob
of ginger – pale, gooey,
half-baked, naked –
stepped out of the oven.
Where's my son?
The little old man
knocked over his
little old chair, kick-boxed
the gob to the ground
and piped quickly
with the icing forcer
a dress on her, rather messy,
and a hat and a handbag
all white, like White Sunday.
In her new clobber
the gob knocked
with one sweet mitt (lacy)
the little old man
to kingdom come.
Out of my way, it said,
then rose up, a tree
of cookie, and surged
like Birnam Wood
on washday at the pa
out the kitchen door.
It was Gingerbread Mama.
They heard her say,
out the side of her

wrinkled raisin lips,
He thinks he can run
but he can't he can't.

3b

A shiny cow trotting out
in her Ted Hughes tuxedo
(but a girl, so like Ellen)
said Gingerbread Boy
looked good enough to eat.
Gingerbread Boy recited
blankly as if from some
Jungian memory
I can run from a woman,
I can run from a man, I can run from you I can I can.
In the mauve distance
an explosion like fireworks
blooming and growing
(like edelweiss, so also
like a flower) and cracking
was Gingerbread Mama.
You can't you can't,
she chanted. *Your asthma.*
That's right, mooched the cow,
he can't, he can't, he's
only good for eating.
Gingerbread Mama turned her
doughy gaze on the cross-
dressing cow. *What*
did you say about my son?
The cow shuddered
from neck to udder.
There was a cattle stop

like the pipes of an organ
exhausted after Bach's
Toccata and Fugue
lying down for a rest.
In the ditch underneath
after a hit from Gingerbread
Mama's mitt the cow rested
in peace and Gingerbread Boy
stopped running and walked
along the road, and
Gingerbread Mama
followed. *I told you so,*
where's your inhaler?

3c

A horse bursting with rump
rippled his billboard teeth
and said Gingerbread Boy
looked just as sweet
as a sugar lump. Here we go,
groaned Gingerbread Boy,
run from a woman, run from a man, run from a cow, run from you I can I can.
A quick shadow, round,
diffuse like a partial
eclipse fell over
rump, mane, nostrils,
hooves. Foam flecked
the horse's flank
(the fs a coincidence);
You can't you can't,
said Gingerbread Mama.
Exactly, whinnied the horse.
Gingerbread Mama

loomed like sunblock.
Was I talking to you?
The horse went all
Pixar – toothy, hoofy.
Think you're cute? said
Gingerbread Mama.
Her icing dress swished
as she mounted
in one white movement,
holding her hat and bag,
the horse, and she rode it
like Pippi Longstocking
except heavier, and so
swaybacked, crazily
into the next chapter.
Gingerbread Boy,
puffed from running,
slowed down
to a walk.

3d

For twelve threshers
raising the pretty husks
that gave them lung cancer
as sunlight hung obliquely
in the golden shed,
it was smoko time
which meant more cancer
and tea and biscuits.
They filed into the field.
The sun was ultra. One
thresher lighting up saw
Gingerbread Boy passing

and said in passing he looked
good enough to eat.
(Note the *enough* – coy,
coining a phrase, that's all.)
Gingerbread Boy didn't
get the metaphor, nor
know that he could
rot your teeth. He did
the can-can routine:
run from a woman, man, cow, horse, run from you, I can I can.
Twelve times (not really).
The twelve threshers –
stubbed their cigarettes
ominously, *on your marks,*
but just for the chase,
like fox and hounds.
Just then Gingerbread Mama's
buttery face appeared
like a daylight moon,
blank, big, serious.
You can't you can't.
But he can, said a thresher,
he said he could. *Don't*
you contradict me, said
Gingerbread Mama.
The threshers shrugged
and tipped their dregs
and moseyed back to the
beautiful cancery shed
and threshed till knock-off time.
Gingerbread Boy sauntered
away, his hips fat from
lack of exercise.
Gingerbread Mama
tromped after him

on her sweet feet
nodding her white hat
and in her head planned
for Gingerbread Boy to run
around the rotary clothesline
at dusk for fitness
while her white dress
dried in the wind.

3e

Before the threshers
could thresh the wheat
twelve mowers
had had to mow it,
so here the story
gets just a little
arse over elbow.
All the same the field
shimmered in the wind
like a Wyeth painting
painted in New Zealand,
and therefore the air,
instead of being burnished
was *like polished silver*,
so beautiful you'd think
nothing could ruffle it
but think again because
Gingerbread Boy.
One of the mowers
was scanning *his world*
when he saw a brown boy
enter into it. He looks
good to eat, he remarked

(no *enough* – he really meant it).
The other mowers
looked and saw
that it was true
and downed tools
to give chase.
Gingerbread Boy
made a fragrant sigh
and twisted his mitts
as best he could:
I've run from a woman,
I've run from a man,
I've run from a cow,
I've run from a horse,
I've run from some threshers, and I can run from you, I can, I –
Gingerbread Boy stopped.
What? said the mowers.
The air crackled, clouds
gathered on the silver
horizon. Gingerbread Mama's
iced hand fell heavily
on Gingerbread Boy's
brown shoulder. *You can't,*
she said. I kn-kn-ow,
said Gingerbread Boy.
(But stuttering
isn't caused by
mothers with big mitts.)
Hanging his head
like Billy Bibbit
Gingerbread Boy
stumbled through
the field of wheat.
The mowers took
a butcher's at

Gingerbread Mama's
icing handbag, her
half-formed undercooked
expression, and turned
to admiring the Wyeth
horizon (in silver),
and parted like a sea
for Gingerbread Boy
to walk through
and went back
to mowing.
Gingerbread Mama
pursed her doughy lips
with certainty.

3f

And finally Gingerbread
Boy came to a river.
A red fox bobbed
like blood near the bank.
He smiled and said,
welcome aboard,
want to cross over
to the other side?
N-Not particularly,
said Gingerbread Boy.
Well, said Red Fox,
jump on my tail anyway.
He had a sleek snout
and glassy eyes like a
fox fur from 1920.
Why would I do that?
asked Gingerbread Boy.

For fun, said Red Fox.
Gingerbread Boy stood
on the boardwalk, arms
folded. F-fun? he said.
Fun, said Red Fox,
paddling to and fro
annoyingly for Ginger-
bread Boy (and for us).
You're making me
dizzy, said Gingerbread Boy.
C'mon, said Red Fox,
doing lengths
of the bathtub
in his head. Admit it,
you're a gingerbread peg
in a round hole. Be
what you want, be
a cowboy, a boy racer,
be Hell Boy, be Waterboy.
Gingerbread Boy shook
his head crisply. But
he did wonder – what if
the little old woman
afflicted with the
cookie-cutter hands
had had round hands
or square hands or
scissor hands. He'd be
a banker, or a lost soul
like Edward in that film.
The randomness of birth.
And also, added Red Fox,
while we're talking
climb onto my back.
A gingerbread peg

in a round hole. I can't,
croaked Gingerbread Boy.
Can't? said Red Fox.
Can't? You most
certainly *can*. No really,
said Gingerbread Boy,
you don't know me,
I can't. Just then
the rickety planks
of the boardwalk
bounced and squeaked.
Red Fox stopped
his watery pacing,
and lifted his snout
out of the water.
Gingerbread Boy twisted
his brittle neck sideways
(a slice, a few cells
wide), and together
he and Red Fox watched
as Gingerbread Mama,
adjusting her sugar hat,
got bigger and bigger.
Red Fox's glassy eyes
grew as dazed as if
they'd come from a furrier.
He licked his thin lips.
Gingerbread Mama
got closer and closer
until she covered
the whole screen
and Red Fox, staring up
from the water, saw
that she was not only big
but half-baked, rouxy,

like cookie dough, just
how he liked it –
Gingerbread Mama
looked good to eat.
Did I hear you say,
said Gingerbread Mama,
the word can
to my son? No ma'am,
said Red Fox, his head
blurry with denial.
Gingerbread Boy
would've blushed
if he could've. He
folded his arms
and looked at the sky.
He remembered the word
unanswering from a poem.
Red Fox said to the Mama,
May I offer you a ride
to the other side?
What's over there?
asked Gingerbread Mama.
She shaded her eyes
at the diaphanous distance.
Peace, said Red Fox.
Any little old women?
asked Gingerbread Mama.
No ma'am, said Red Fox
(he was American).
Any little old men? No ma'am.
Any cows? No ma'am.
Any horses? No ma'am.
Any threshers? No ma'am.
Any mowers? No ma'am.
Gingerbread Mama put

her gingerbread mitt
to her raisin mouth
(almost nibbled it!),
pondered a bit, turned
to Gingerbread Boy
who was cooling
his oven-fresh heels
on the boardwalk.
I'll go, you follow, said
Gingerbread Mama,
and bring your inhaler.
Red Fox's eyes gleamed.
Jump on my tail – well
maybe not jump, climb
carefully. As Gingerbread
Boy watched Gingerbread
Mama roll onto Red Fox's
toetoe tail he thought of
The Submerged Cathedral,
plus the water tinkled
musically. There was
a giggle and Gingerbread
Mama climbed onto
Red Fox's back which
was better, like an iceberg,
the ninety-per-cent-submerged
cathedral. Climb onto
my shoulder, said Red Fox.
Not too heavy? trilled
Gingerbread Mama. Not
in the least, said Red Fox.
Soon Gingerbread Mama
was fifty per cent submerged
like a boat. Red Fox said,
Climb onto my nose. Oh,

said Gingerbread Mama,
get away with you.
Gingerbread Boy watched
as Gingerbread Mama
strained and flopped
onto Red Fox's snout.
As she teetered there,
Red Fox snapped her up.
It took a lot of snapping.
Half-way through, Red Fox
paused to wipe his chops
and say, This certainly
is a supersized meal.
Just before the end
Gingerbread Mama raised
her one remaining body part,
her face, and said,
*You shouldn't swim for
thirty minutes after eating.*
And with that her sugary
buttery cheeks dissolved
in the stream, and the raisin
sank. As small fish
gooped up the crumbs
Red Fox clutched
his cramping stomach
and cried out in agony.
A moment later the waters
closed over Red Fox.
Gingerbread Boy stood
alone on the boardwalk.
It had been quite a day.
Born from the oven
of the little old woman
and the little old man

only that morning –
before Gingerbread Mama
which took some getting
your head around
and made you think of
the notion of devolution.
Then there was the cow, the horse, the twelve threshers, the twelve mowers,
who would've wolfed him
down, he supposed, if he
hadn't run, or if Gingerbread
Mama hadn't whatever.
Gingerbread Boy felt
a pang of grief,
elemental, reminiscent
of the floury board. It'd been
a brief acquaintance,
but she was still his mother
if you turned the world
on its head, which we did
in the southern hemisphere.
At the end of the boardwalk
was a bus stop. Gingerbread
Boy went and waited
at it. He didn't know
where he was going.
He didn't know why
he'd been running.
(Why not just disappear
like a round cookie?)
He didn't know why
he'd stopped running.
Gingerbread Boy
looked up at the sky.
Well it ain't no use sitting
wondering why, babe,

he sang to himself,
if'n you don't know by now.
Presently a bus came
and Gingerbread Boy
got on it. Welcome aboard,
said the bus driver,
a rooster who didn't look
quite nice, but Gingerbread
Boy took a seat anyway.
The bus pulled out
from the strand and
thundered off through
the streets of the city
into the countryside.
There were no stops.
The bus kept going
and going. Gingerbread Boy
never got eaten, neither
did he die. When you
have grown old
and your children
have grown old
and your grandchildren
have grown old
Gingerbread Boy
will still be riding the bus
to nowhere.

THE WEDDING RING LOST TO THE SEA
AND OTHER STORIES

1.

A man shook hands with the sea,
one organism to another, present and passing.

You could see him a mile off
snorkelling like a whale with his spouting

mammal children. It was piss-easy for the sea
to help herself to his silver with a fine thread of gold

ring from a jeweller in Kingsland
the finger

thinned lately from work and sunlight
and turn away humming, merely (la mer!)

going about her business, as if
the ring were her pet stripey

tropical fish she'd nursed from an amoeba
all these millennia. The man said to the sea

Have it, if it means that much to you.
I feel sorry for you, I have

the woman. And the sea
her feelings wounded slightly

like a gash to her stone surface
wore the ring

which reflected the light of her estranged moon
right down to its bright grains of sand.

2.

A woman swimming back then
aged ten (a late starter)

nearly drowned in the cold Marist
Newtown Pool. No one noticed

she got to the point, quite profound,
of saying to herself in her head

(because the water) I am going now.

Triumphant moment of clasping
death as the better option.

And she went into this place.
She will tell you, apart from

the first few minutes when the water wants to make
a blue inlet of your lungs, sheltered,

and you want it the way it's always been
but there's no stopping progress

and small craft sail in and wait out
a storm, it's not such a bad way to go

or place to go. Don't worry!

Now the husband knows his wife,
their bodies grown together like coral reef

and rock, will never venture out beyond
her waist.

3.

A whale had that sinking feeling
so kicked phosphorous about
like a football. It was still blue, so it sang

high-soprano songs of its feats
and disappointments, fa-la-la.
This worked to some extent

to ward off melancholy, to pass the time
and water, which weighed heavily.
It was either that or give up and go home.

Home was a long way away and, frankly,
out of the question. You have to hand it
to the whale. Let's not forget humanity.

Here we are, plunging about on the earth
breathing in its foreign air
and telling ourselves all about it.

4.

As if dusting
the sitting room

she lifts each swimmer
puts it back

on the same little worked
mat. Sometimes

she pockets
one or two

or three, from ennui,
and never fails to be

surprised by the uproar
(there are so many)

tiny when seen from
eternity.

5.

A boy came down to the sea
with this friend the cigarette for company

whose walk was a pact with a fighting dog
hating and loving. He set out

across the mudflats, which stretched
through no fault of the sea, a whole K

towards the distant shore. The boy
said to his dog (if he'd had a dog),

This sea is not even blue. I can walk to Te Atatu.
The sea, sensitive but no more than

anyone said, That girl on the beach.
Beach? Well, concrete wall.

Which I will mount at sunset.
I will drive her away. Watch.

The boy tossed his cigarette hissing
at the sea and with his dog

went to the place where
the mud and water first become one.

FORTY YEARS OF HABITATION

For love has fairly drove me silly – hoping you're the same!
– Jack Judge, 'It's a Long Way to Tipperary'

His dream:
Under the tarpaulin of his face he's fumbling with matches.
A flare. I watch its history (young, at least
so far). It rains outside, enough to swell the river.
I might come in.

His span:
I had an another idea and that was
he'd be the mountains and I'd be the long white cloud.

His face:
My outstretched hands inevitably encountered how things feel.
Since then I have carried it everywhere with me.

His weight:
No weight.
No, no weight.

His profile:
My finger delineated the giant. I said I will go up and down
and he turned to face me.
Oh no! Where is it?

His hair:
My nose and mouth
amphibian: air and his hair.

His volume:
When someone occupies most of a bed
despite a treaty
you still consider the occupied bit
yours.

His volume:
Speak loudly because I am a little deaf.
Little bit. This then is about
his voice, not my reception.
I like it.
I said I like it.

His thighs:
A long time ago I saw a man lying under a car fixing it.
I came home.

His calves:
I have likened them to Captain Cook's after three voyages to the Antipodes
pacing the deck but going nowhere,
as on an exercycle.
He has the good fortune of already being down here,
obviously.

His thumb:
The pocket
between the ball of my foot and the heel. It largely contains air.
I didn't know it was there before.

His fever:
This happens seldom, is years in the planning.
When it comes it is a perfect island, still,
self-contained. I take over the thinking temporarily.
Books, discs. How lucky
he is.

His puku:
He's fond of it and gives it treats, so it has grown up to be affectionate.
There's a heart in there,
not a heart, a centre.

His hands:
Hands can be so foreign. Sometimes
I am shocked by hands. But these hands are
native to the body. They grow big
in summer.

His arms:
Ditto the arms, more or less,
except they can lift boxes.

His penis:
A maypole (not to be too
Eurocentric). I plait
my arms and legs
in a complicated fashion.

His shoulders:
are poets. Tell everything
by gesture.

His eyes:
The depth of them initially a challenge.
I hadn't been in past my waist since a near-drowning experience as a child.
Also, they read a lot of material.

57

His material:
Here's a one-cell-wide cross-section as of 11 a.m.:
Samoan Material Culture, by Te Rangi Hiroa.
Will give you some idea.

His brain:
therefore, is colourful, like a library or railway station
or bazaar or wall
of the people.

His back:
He doesn't know much about his back, so there is no
history of his back. I could make up anything.
In fact I will
one day.

His soul:
Where to start? I suppose it propels
all of the above. Maybe I am
out of my depth here. Help!

His feet:
The feet are actually pivotal. Sometimes they swell painfully.
I could almost say 'like a nineteenth-century bishop'.
But that's quite unfair.
'Twenty-first-century bishop.'

His walk:
All of it is a distraction from the true nature of the feet which are big
and powerful, plates of meat,
but tender, absorbent, with movable parts,
the tectonics that move
the man
and keep the man on the ground

Have I:
(Yes, me.)
forgotten anything?

His birthday:
Ah. Happy birthday. I think. I must say I was expecting
some sort of continuity but now I see
from its location
that this birthday is different from the last and from the one before that
and I'm not sure what to say about it,
I'm not sure that happy birthday is appropriate

His copy:
for a copy
which may or may not bear any relation to the original.
For instance the original occurred

His travels:
in a fixed place
but there is no guarantee – never was, it turns out –
that subsequent birthdays
will be in that place. They can roam
at will
out into the world and be celebrated

His sense of smell:
in strange ports
where new-smelling flowers grow and complicated insects
fly out suddenly from behind bookcases
and buildings remain calm
as if everything were normal.
If the birthdays can be removed
so far from the original birthday

His knowledge:
then the man, I think
needs to redefine 'ground' as
anything that he happens to find at that moment under his feet.
He needs to redefine 'brain' according to the new knowledge
in it, and this is knowledge he never sought out,
it just came into the brain.

His expression:
He redefines
'profile' as something that changes its outline depending on
the expression, and is filled in variously with beads, shells,
with climbing plants, guests. He redefines
'face', or I do,

His face:
because I touched it. I had taken it everywhere with me
fingered it blindly in my pocket
like some kind of talisman,
but when I looked at it again
I saw it was transient, the features
flickering like a years-long series of photographs posted
on YouTube, and in the end alarmingly

His glance down:
forgettable. (I have forgotten
the face of my dead brother, for instance.) He redefines
'thumbs' because when he looks down and sees them

His 'like':
lying in his lap
the thumbs lying in his lap
are like hermit crabs in a new place,
where he has taken them.

His body temperature:
It is the same for other parts of his body.
His 'fever', which came so rarely, inhabited his body for the years
he lived near the equator
and raised its temperature by a degree
so that he seemed less hot
by comparison with his surroundings.

His surprise:
He didn't ask for this change in temperature
or necessarily want it, it just happened.
He redefines 'have' as nothing,

His other surprise:
and finally he redefines 'dream'
which he had thought, because it was subject to history,
could at least be relied upon
like the original birthday
to be fixed

His realisation:
but his dream turns out to have no bearing on anything
even less than any of the other attributes

His footstep:
his dream turns out to be an introduced species
with no predictability beyond a random crazing of possibilities
which crack and fan out into the world
with a seemingly malevolent
energy, although it isn't malevolent, it is trying
to do good
because if in the beginning there was no dream
how would anyone plan the next footstep?

His dream:
Without his dream he would constantly look back
to see if he had forgotten anything.
He would wonder about living
all these years in his own body.
He would wonder if the sum of the parts,
the face, hands, shoulder, soul, the rare fever,
the lost birthdays,
amounted to anything
or whether it was just dust
and that in the end he might walk away from it
like a farmer from
his wrath.
If he had no dream he might float upwards
because there was nothing heavy,
arms, legs, torso. He might
fly apart because there was
no centre, no puku
connecting the other things.
And in the end he knows for certain
(or I do, who loves him)
that the least concrete thing
the thing that is so light it isn't even there
holds the heaviness together.

LOSTLING AND FOUNDLING

1. Buying a Phone

Day and night you are dressed in the heat.
Before this you were naked. All your life, not a stitch
of warmth apart from your clothes. Birds
on the grass roost close to the underground
power lines. You have a new lightness.
At night the kids on the lawn rush headlong
into the corner of their eye, where toads hop
and they count them. *I have numbered every one*

of my toads. Sometimes twice. The toads forget
they have already jumped. In the empty apartment
the phone is the first piece of furniture, hopeful,
seeks daylight, a tendency to weep. No – beep,
you idiot! At this point you have the wild idea
it will find what it is looking for.

2. Work

The most-asked question is do your cocktails have
umbrellas in them? It's true that here we have learned
to make Pineapple Bombers. But no. That thing
on the rim of the glass is the sun going down
on America. When I first looked out from Waikiki
I thought I was seeing the Pacific Ocean
for the first time. People think we lie
under umbrellas at the beach all the time,

but no. Mostly life goes on just the same. I am
still planning my book, *Talking Loudly: A Self-Help Guide
for Better Communication between the Members
of Rock Bands.* Seeing a need which has not diminished
with distance. I am reading narrowly just as I always did,
a sharp point under which there is no shade.

3. Trade Wind

If I hung up the washing to dry outside I would be
white trash, and I wouldn't mind that. I am a Haole
but I have my Bachelor of Music to comfort me.
The truth is there is nowhere to hang it, so I tumble
through the warm wind dragging the white sheets
behind me in a cart to where the breeze is domesticated
like a cat. It chases its tail. The clothes are songs
without words. If I found the coin dispenser empty

of harpsichord music in F which is the key
four quarters fall in, a beautiful tinkle (a dollar a download,
but beware, always the same tune), well first I'd curse
the manager and second look for coins on the floor.
If I saw one (I did once) I would leap on it.
Two coins are worth their weight in wind.

4. Flood, Halloween, 2004

What daughter put on her bed in case water came in
the door: violin (in case), 25 stuffed animals (in suitcase),
Harry Potter books (in cardboard case), Harry Potter DVDs
(in cases). What I put on son's bed for son who was trapped
at the school dance: electric guitar (in hard case), small amp
(in soft case), electronic games (in case), ceremonial Samoan
fishing stick (no case). What husband put on bed in case water
came in the door: motherboard (no case). What I put:

this, this, this, this, this, this, this, this, this, this
this, this, this, this, this, this, this, this, this
this, this, this, this, this, this, this, this
this, this, this, this, this, this, this, this, this
this, this, this, this, this, this, this, this, this, this, this
this, this, this, this, this, this, this, in case.

5. Vase

I wasn't looking for a vase but I found a vase in the Red
Cross shop. Blue, six inches high, vase-shaped. Up close
I saw that it was crazed. It cost a dollar. At home,
cradling its swell, its pouting upper lip, I inspected
the bottom. Eric Juckert in a loopy scrawl. I Googled him.
From Shepparton, Australia (where John comes from, someone
I used to know), active in the fifties, collectible. My vase
was worth $40. I have a few things back home, family things,

a silver tea-set, English china, small dark side-tables
carved by a great-aunt. I think of them sometimes sitting
in their bright/dark New Zealand light. I look at my blue vase,

which I first saw among cut glass in the junk shop. It doesn't stop
night coming on suddenly. I never knew I would have
a vase in Honolulu. If it broke I would be upset.

6.

The line of light along his young clean hair
gone haywire in the bell of his trumpet as if he'd ruffled
a yellow dog there. Collars to be worn on
the evening of. In the school cafeteria – *no student
will leave* – a swaggering When the Saints was
forced through an aperture, a hole in a hedge, a new world
on the other side. How they love war and cabaret
here, I said, and saw him politely empty his condensed breath.

Crossing the bridge on hot afternoons coming from
the supermarket I'd heard him practise. The notes
long-sighted among the shopping. The bridge over the stream
that flooded and washed three parked cars
into the branches of the trees. The trumpet they opened up
at customs revealing its deep blue velvet wound.

7.

as if her notes had formed in the womb like milk
teeth otherwise where did they come from? There were
CDs all about, so many Saturns. Once she heard
a real girl play the sound of a possum trapped
in a church hall – wood, copper, hair, rosin – and wanted

in. Today they played Suzuki Book Four
at the mall – girls an aloha dress, boys ditto shirt –
while tourists shopped and the canal drew

its whole long arm down to Waikiki. Sometimes like the tide
she is sick of it. She laughed when Brian Potiki asked,
Do you learn Kooki Method? In the end it is
something to get through, the restless afternoon
of a childhood illness or ecstasy. The odd pockmark,
a half-note that will never leave her.

8. My Address is Flight 10 to Honolulu

In the sky I forgot everything, which was probably for the best
– like childbirth, no going back. A grey hand rushed into
a grey glove. I found we had brought our own brightness. Then
living as gods (because frankly who else gets up here?)
minus an engineer who said even engineers don't know how
we stay airborne – but otherwise fine, wine, song, a film,
a talk with the window at sunset, in fact a bit of an epic,
all the sex and all the death, all the love, all the utu.

Phew! I pictured a little life down there, in that darkness.
I'd read the ephemera in *the pocket in the seat in front of you*
– scent, linen, summer, the clamour of children clear
as bells. A smiling husband. A house to put them in. I was
as good as a god or little artist. At midnight I swear
it all came roaring up to greet me.

9. Realisation in Mānoa, for Some Reason

There was the flood. Once the city waterways had packed up
they ended up pumping raw sewage into the Ala Wai Canal.
A man fell into it and died from the infection. It was
Ash Wednesday. I always took the kids to Mass, these Eastery
Christmastimes – see the baby, the corpse, etc. They were even
baptised. Of course I don't *believe* it. Jesus! But let me have
my Irish marae, won't you? Let the children pack
morning and evening I have no other food but my grief

into their bags. It might prove useful when compared with
heartbreak. But I have watched the debauched
war and read the concordance of the bishop. I have talked
to the walking wounded from the boys' schools and finally
believe them. And I am sick. The thing is
I only ever wanted the bathwater.

10. Green Card

If you came in through Ellis Island your medical exam
took six seconds and was free. You went ashore with your
good lungs and disappeared into America. We now know
we don't have and have not been in contact with TB.
We now know we are unlikely to contract mumps, measles,
rubella or tetanus. We knew all along how our parents died
but now we know we will probably go that way too (why else
ask). I know I don't have breast cancer. The menfolk

know they don't have testicular cancer. We now know
we don't have syphilis or AIDS. We can have unsafe sex
with anyone in America. We now know we are happy. It was

noted that we are not addicted to any substances. We took
a thousand dollars in greenbacks with us to the doctor. They only
accept cash because afterwards we will disappear into America.

11. My 40,000-Word Thesis on Atonality in *the bone people*

Atonality is the absence of a pitch centre in music. Atonal music is
homeless. Poor atonal music. But wait! There is much research in
the field of music-in-literature. And lots of music in *the bone people*:
refs to existing music, allusions to tonalities, and use of sound (i.e., it's poetic).
What I found: *bp*'s tonal music is often shattered by homeless pitches.
Do-Re-Mi – Take that! Fa-So-La – Arghh! Ti-Do – Mmph!
My thesis is accompanied by a CD I'm rather proud of. '*the bone people*'s
Found Compositions.' Absolutely brilliant music. She loves her music,

Keri, I kid you not. Sea shanties, flamenco guitar, European folk songs,
waiata. What I wanted to say was, *bp* gets touted as a bicultural novel but
I think it's a Maori novel. My thesis is soft-bound in the Victoria library.
No one will ever read it, but aha – here you are reading this poem!
I should have written my thesis in fourteen lines, shouldn't I?
I just did. Signed, AK, B. Mus., ATCL, MA. Yay!

12. Ligaments

The violin under the bed fell apart one night like a body
sleeping. When she opened the velvet cavity in the morning
the instrument was out of it. Imagine having to be glued together
after dreaming. That's exactly how I feel. We took the violin
to the violin hospital. In the car she cradled the pieces

like a sick dog, or pieces of dog. Tears fell on it. The horsehair
(think paniolo or Big Island ranchers – and yes, pianola)
was okay. So what had happened? Heat plus glue?

I have no clue, as they say here, and now I know why.
Because violins fall apart that's why. Now I know a lot of things.
Why the orchestra room at 'Iolani is so freezing, it's like going back
to New Zealand, why the mangos fizz in the trees, from the sun,
why they hate Haoles, for what they did to Kanaka Maoli
that's why. Why they call fall Fall, because it's America.

13. On Becoming a Turtle

In my fiftieth year I am air-clumsy. My hands are another
pair of feet. I crawl on the floor looking for lost objects.
I used to sew as a hobby. Now threading a needle is Russian roulette.
Gambling is banned in the state of Hawai'i. It was either a casino
or the sea. The sea won. At Haunama Bay you hear people say,
as they point out shapes in the aqua, as on an X-ray, He could be
as much as fifty years old. Or she. My remaining hobbies? I like reading
and tucking myself into my own geometry. I'm learning to breathe

a new element, to move about with a sort of paddling motion.
I tip my head on one side and examine my neck. I remember
bad cases of sunburn. I remember wind. Stories are tangled
all around me. I've realised they are not as distinct from each other
as I once thought. The *he said she saids* – Whoa! as they say
in America, and I say, because I have immigrated here apparently.

14. Daughter and Friends Play with American Girl Dolls

Only one girl owns an American Girl Doll, the bossiest girl.
The other girls look at American Girl Dolls in the catalogue.
They talk about the doll they will have when they have a doll.
Molly, Emily, Jo, or Susan. There are plans for her good life,
the clothes she will wear, where she will sleep, the words
she will say. The dolls are expensive, $89 each plus postage.
There is no store on the island, just wind of. They play
with the text. They are readers. (What you are. Egad!)

There are too many words. One of them must go. American Girl,
American Doll. One time in New York we went to the store
and handled Molly. I said, Buy it, you love American Girl Dolls.
By the time we got home she'd grown out of it. I bought it off her.
I love it. I got it a muumuu on the Big Island – said *fits American
Girl Doll*. I propped her in the hall as if she were dead, I mean alive.

MY CARBON GAZE

1.

Because there were hills to the east and hills to the west, there was a good chance that when you looked at something it would be a hill. Perhaps it would be a hill with a family member or a friend in the foreground. A family member or friend might be called a loved one for short.

2.

With the hills and the loved ones far apart, your eyes would end up making so many trips back and forth that their orbit solidified into a sort of object. It was a wire model of an atom like they had in the museum. Or perhaps a model of the solar system. In any case, a round thing involving energy and with the potential to explode, but that would be in exceptional circumstances. Probably never.

3.

I still have it in my natural history section, although sometimes I wish I didn't. Sometimes I wish I didn't have a natural history section. I wish I hadn't looked up at those hills so often – willy-nilly – between 1960 and 1985, and looked back down at the loved ones, because now I am left with this wire model and it will never go away. In fact it will, because it is organic, but only after a very long time. Perhaps even after I am dead.

4.

Most summers there was a fire on one of the hills, the east or the west, the sun-coming-up hill or the sun-going-down hill. It would seem like the hill was burning, but it was only the gorse. Not so serious. But serious enough to prompt a teacher to set a Poem for homework.

5.

On the way home you could hear the black crackling and it seemed to have a personality, and not a very nice one.

6.

My mother wrote the poem quickly as she peeled the potatoes – in fact she only said it. I wrote it in my McCahon handwriting but much more neatly. *Of English descent it crowds the hills, / Originally meant for hedges and sills. / A prickly maze, a funeral pyre / a golden haze, a monstrous fire.*

7.

There was only ever one hill on fire at a time. The problem would be if both hills caught fire at the same time, and the fires might burn down into the valley, and the trees would burn, and the lawns, and all our houses and their contents. And our Prefaces and Introductions. Not to mention the people. But we would run down to the beach. That's what we would do.

8.

There was an article in the paper about the possibility of a tidal wave sweeping up the bay and taking everything with it, and if you hadn't gone in the earthquake that preceded the tidal wave, you would now be finished off altogether. This was the opposite of the fire. You would be washed the other way, all the way into town. How extreme the world was. Why not something in the middle?

9.

(Why not fear something in the middle? Earth, wind, a few other things.)

10.

And the hills were mostly benign anyway. They were just there, like your name. You might even get sick of them, of looking up at them and back again. Why don't people get sick of their name? Maybe they do. Maybe they say, If I hear that name one more time I'll scream.

11.

Sometimes you might look up at the hills and think, **I am looking at the hills,** and you might have some sort of reaction, e.g., **They are dark against the white sky and are very beautiful.** Or, **They have a sun like a solitaire nestled into them, but not for long. See look – gone! Divorced. I told you so.** These kinds of reactions were the first attempts to connect the hills and the people in the foreground. But it is probably impossible. Well nigh impossible.

12.

In spring they were brassy yellow with gorse flowers. In summer they were 'tinder dry' (a cliché) and 'brown' (not a cliché because the word brown doesn't have much to it and people haven't got sick of it yet). Okay, brown.

13.

When both sides of the hills were brown, to the east and the west, in the 'height of summer', a fire might be lit by a boy letting off fire-crackers saved from Guy Fawkes, or by a girl letting off fire-crackers (svd fr. GF), or by a man going for a walk on the Town Belt and smoking a cigarette, or by a woman (gng fr wlk on TB w. cig.), and the fire brigade would be called out.

14.

But because there were two fires – one lit by the boy or the man, the other lit by the girl or the woman – the fire brigade would have no chance of taking control, and the fire would burn down into the valley. And everyone, family members and friends (loved ones for short as there would not be much time), would run down the Parade to the beach, and go and stand in the sea because there would be nowhere else to go. I am still out there. I am standing in the cold sea at Island Bay and it is 2011, and it is freezing, and I am waiting for the fires on the hills to go out.

HELLO KITTY, GOODBYE PICCADILLY

Imagine you'd come to Hawai'iki early.
                              I don't have Hawai'iki.
Imagine you were in Heaven.
                              I don't have Heaven.
Imagine you were in Paradise
                    but at first you don't recognise Paradise,
        or smell it or touch it,
                      because you miss earth too much,
and being earthly.
                You miss the cold wind and you wish
that instead of leaning into it
                    reading it with your mouth
and casting it aside like small-talk
        on all those occasions of cold wind
                    you had gathered it up
and kept it in a suitcase. Then you could
            carry it with you to the new place
open it there
          and remember what cold wind feels like.
You say to yourself
        if only I had done that
            cold wind would come rushing back
but you didn't.
        In Paradise it is so hot your teeth
            loosen and creak in your gums
and your hands hum.
        You notice dainty sandals, gold dresses
shirts accumulating on a lawn
           red birds.
      You remember a coat, olive green, rough,

sea-going you wore
        near the sea. The beach wall was scooped out by waves,
and kelp rotted
        in your nostrils.
                You wore your coat to Mass where the squeak
of new pine pews
           rang out into the still air above the people
                   like modern bells
and you cricked your neck to engage with
          the baleful mosaic stare of the Jesus.
There was a department store
        where the air sprang with grey wool.
That was where your wore the coat
           but can't recall the exact nature
     of how you needed it.
Imagine you'd come to Hawai'iki early.
           I don't have Hawai'iki.
Imagine you were in Heaven.
       I don't have Heaven.
           Imagine you were in Paradise
and one day in Paradise
       when you haven't been there long
you look up and find streetlights swimming
         and people talking at an aquarium
and the jellyfish are purple
      and pulse like a heart.
After a day of hard light
     dusk falls suddenly
        as if the dark were heavy
and the stream that flows close to your apartment
       becomes wetter and shinier
in the moonlight.
          You can't help recalling
that you once climbed aboard a bus
      perfunctorily, like pecking

                              an old relative
but you threw it away.
                    You watch the news
                              on and off
and the accent of the newsreader bounces
                                        in loping kilohertz
but over time dies down
                    until you lose it somewhere inside your ear.
                              You hear
your own accent,
          which used to be beyond hearing, a dog's whistle.
                              Imagine you were in Paradise
and in that Paradise you notice
                    that the sea is cloudy with sunblock
and rushes up the beach tinkling with the gold rings
                                        of newlyweds,
          and the metal detectors of the homeless
are made very happy.
                    The hills thrust up sharply,
dark, and cars burrow through them
                    like rabbits. You hear someone say
on the warm air that if you take pork
                              over the Pali road
your car will break down
                    and a woman in white will appear
                                        hitch-hiking and you vow
never to do that.
                    It is your first plan in Paradise
if you can count plans
                    in the place you didn't plan to go to
which you think you can.
                              If you look for a book
in a certain section of the Hamilton library
                    a hand will tap you on the shoulder
and late at night in the carpark

of the Walmart where they disturbed the bones
the bones will pick you clean
if you're not careful. You will be
careful in Paradise.
You notice that some days the air is mauve
and thick and someone tells you, kindly,
about vog from the volcanoes
and it makes you dizzy, the information,
the politeness.
The island, the sea, the waterfalls are pretty.
They close the schools on Fridays
and it is hot. With a pang you remember
the nose of a white cat.
Imagine you were in Paradise but when you arrived
you thought it wasn't Paradise.
You remembered crisp air,
cold as a cave. At home you knew someone
who knew someone, a shadow,
and you would say hello.
All day in Paradise you shake hands
with strangers, rabbit ears
on a wall.
You don't know. You don't know.
In Paradise they sound
the emergency siren all over the island
every first of the month, 11.45 a.m. sharp.
You jump out of your skin. It is hot anyway.
You spare a thought for the indentured
plantation workers in their sugarcane cages,
whose great-grandchildren
perform dental surgery at Ala Moana Tower.
There was no shade.
There is no shade.
Rents are high and people say it is the price
of Paradise

79

and others say there should be an excise
                              tax so the children can go back to school on Fridays
although they don't really need school.
                              In Paradise you don't need anything.
You read in the paper that depressed kids
                              are turning up at the Help Program
        with the red-haired gene they need help with
in Paradise.
                              For instance the word 'bong'
echoes through the university shuttle service,
                              and the campus is full of stray cats.
There's a certain peacefulness.
                              Off-ramps with banks of tires,
escape routes for runaway trucks.
                              You clean the bathroom mirror in Paradise
and on the shelf below it
                              a pink Post-it says 'Dialects of Seeing'
in the round writing of your opposite.
                              You don't clean it up.
        You know this is like a dream, this found thing,
so ho-hum – no human
                              endeavour. You didn't make this up. You couldn't
make this stuff up, but you tell it anyway.
                              Bong bong.
        Imagine you'd come to Hawai'iki early.
                              I don't have Hawai'iki.
Imagine you were in Heaven.
                I don't have Heaven.
Imagine you were in Paradise
                              and on arrival
you remember what you had been told about Paradise
                              at the little old cold school:
In Paradise you will sit for a long time
                looking at everything as if for the first time
and you will understand.

You realise that you like

           the sing-song of Pidgin,
an exhibition of empty rooms with carved wooden

           weeds growing out of the skirting boards,
a variety of friendliness.

    Kimchi, mandoo, spicy ahi maki, manapua buns,

           handbags.
(In Paradise you don't need money.

           A handbag is pure luxury.)
You think you see a sign saying Occidental Rugs

           but you're mistaken: your eyesight
which you thought would be fixed

    in Paradise.

           It is dazzling and you are dazzled. The sea.
You walk about. You drive about

           learning the avenues of Paradise.
In the Chinese cemetery on the hill

           the names of the immigrants
under the colonies of lichen

           look out over the bunched handful of city, mini Hong Kong.
You wonder in passing

           about your body, its whereabouts.
Eventually in Paradise you discover a shopping mall.

           This development is a long time coming
because before you came to Paradise

           you bought meat, Brussel sprouts, rough socks.
In the shopping mall goldfish swim in blue ponds

           and perfume coils out of stores to engulf you
and the song composed by the queen

           when she was incarcerated in the palace

    'Aloha 'Oe'

           deposits its snippets in the warm air.
You stop at certain shops,

           and you learn them, and you like them
for their sound and smell

and their meaning gathers

                      like clouds which when heavy

fall onto the carpark, and gather again.

        And again you process along the upper level of the mall

and warm air bathes your feet

             and you incline your head towards price tags

and you fall in love with a cat-face

               and stroke a purse in its likeness

to have and to hold.

        Imagine you were in Paradise

             and in Paradise a funny expression

sometimes pops out of your mouth

         and your children laugh because

      nobody says that

           here. (And here

you need to add that for your children

           this is not Paradise because for them

there is only childhood.)

          You realise with a jolt that your children's DNA

does not contain the expressions your parents used,

           that you use,

and if they took a sample of tissue from your children

         they would not be able to prove relationship

through *work cut out, mind you,*

         time being.

On the way to the supermarket you see a film crew

          shooting *Lost* out of a white trailer.

By the side of the road you see papery leaves

             a layer of chlorophyll.

       You try to remember the shape of the hills

that you looked at every day for twenty years,

         their greenness, blackness, orangeness

      but the only things that come are words

and so you put them down

         and they will have to do.

But the hills were always going to go anyway.
                                                And the words.
You try to remember the theme music to the news you watched
        before Paradise,
                        the trumpets important like Yeomen,
but it falls through your fingers,
                                which doesn't matter because it was always
going to become unimportant anyway.
        In Paradise you try to remember
                                a tune your father used to sing while shaving.
        I dream of Jeanie with the light brown hair,
but it is lost. You find
                that in order to remember *It's a long way to Tipperary*
you need seagulls to be cawing overhead,
                        bells to be ringing out the Angelus,
your breath to be white on the air
                                as you run down the passage to your parents' room,
school uniform bundled in your arms,
        you need to be doing up the rubber buttons on your woollen vest
while the gas fire snorts.
        The song would never have lasted anyway.
                                In Paradise you walk
down McCarthy Mall
                between the acacia trees and their geisha
sprinklers,
                and you swing your briefcase because you have a job
in a place and you think
                        western capitalism meets eastern cat
and discard it immediately   83
                        because thoughts are like that
                                and this is Paradise.
Warmth rises through your body
                        and you realise that you are cool
and the balconies of apartment blocks downtown
        look like box seats for the Pacific Ocean

and for the Sun King, and you want
to wave from one, your fan, your beauty spot
                    and that the creaky wooden villa with light
coming through the floorboards
                        that you had lived in on earth
has fallen away, and you smile
            at the thought of the bright new friends you've made.
                                    The school you went to
topples into the cold gully below it, and magpies rise oodle-ardling
                    until they are full stops
and the extinct varieties of Hawai'i
                            fill your bookshelves.
A cat you knew once
        who slept in your bed on cold nights with its face poking out
becomes mythical,
                but you were always going to outlive it anyway,
and a cousin on your mother's side falls away
                    but she was always elusive.
There is no brother
            but a digital camera, no aunt
                            but a pair of shoes,
there are no grandparents but a hair straightener,
                            but they were always
going. There is no coat,
                but you were always going to lose it,
there is no cold wind,
            but it was always going to be forgotten anyway
because of the nature of cold and of wind.
                        When you travel on the bus you are
a little chilly in the air conditioning,
            and you listen to the voice announcing each stop
in well-articulated Hawaiian.
You know whose voice it is and you feel like turning
            to the old Japanese woman next to you and saying,
I've met that man! You know people

in Paradise. You remember the voice
from all the previous occasions of going on the bus
of which there are many now because you have been
quite a long time in Paradise,
and the voice is familiar
and comforting,
and when you get off the bus
warmth rises through your body
and it rises through your body and it rises
through your body, and you see
and you feel
that you had to go some time
and that this is Paradise.

NOTES

'The Darling North' owes much to *Old New Zealand* (1863), by Frederick E. Maning, the 2001 edition edited by Alex Calder (Leicester UP), and to *North* (1975) by Seamus Heaney (Faber, 1996).

Maning was an Irish national who lived in Tasmania as a child, and in the Hokianga from 1833. He traded with Maori, referred to himself as a 'Pakeha-Maori', and owned 200 acres at Onoke on the south side of the Hokianga Harbour. He ran a successful timber and trading business in the north. Maning was reportedly anti-Treaty, but in the 1860s sat as a judge in the Land Court. He married Moengaroa of Te Hikutu, a hapu of Nga Puhi, and had four children.

The following quotations are from *Old New Zealand*: *I have now all New Zealand to caper about in* . . . (p. 110); . . . *and so, putting on the most unconcerned countenance* . . . (p. 100); *I can hardly understand how it is that I have not yet landed* (p. 99); *I get so confused. I feel just as if I was two different persons* . . . (p. 198).

Quotations from *North* are as follows: *A love-nest is disturbed* ('Kinship', p. 35); *the slime kingdoms* ('Strange Fruit', p. 34); *sowed with the mouthing corpses* . . . ('Ocean's Love to Ireland', p. 40); *no treaty I foresee will salve* . . . ('Act of Union', pp. 43–44); *mother ground sour with the blood of her faithful* ('Kinship', p. 38).

Other references that appear in this text are gratefully acknowledged: *The Navigator* on page 7 is the feature film by Vincent Ward. The Augustus Earle painting on page 21 is *View of the Village of Parcuneigh and the Entrance of the E-O-Ke-Angha River, New Zealand*. The 'polished silver' light on page 41 is from *Towards Another Summer*, by Janet Frame (Vintage, 2007, p. 12). The lyrics on pages 49–50 are from 'Don't Think Twice, It's All Right', by Bob Dylan. The filled-in profiles on page 60 are from the photographer Jocelyn Carlin's *To Be: Portraits*. The riddle on page 73 really was composed by my mother, Veronica Kennedy, c. 1967. The song 'Aloha 'Oe' (p. 81) was composed by the Hawaiian queen Lili'uokalani.

Thanks to the team at Auckland University Press – Katrina Duncan, Christine O'Brien and especially Anna Hodge for extraordinary advice. Thanks to Mary Paul for enlightening conversations about Maning.

And of course love and thanks to Robert Sullivan.